Chronic Defiance
R.C. Lloyd

Praise for Chronic Defiance

"R.C. Lloyd has crafted a collection like no other. Her words are stardust in the universal experience of those who live with chronic illness. Her work shines a light on the unspoken. A testimony of faith amidst suffering, and the freedom found within."

- Erin Forbes, Author of the Fire & Ice book series

"Beautiful, reflective, powerful. Lloyd's poetry weaves joy and sorrow, pain and life. Her words evoke emotion, reminding you of the joys of being alive."

- Sara Francis, Author of Stardust and She Whispered Through The Woods

"R.C. Lloyd poured her soul into these poems full of truth and tenderness...You won't regret opening this book to discover what the author holds in her beautiful core."

- Marina Aimée, Author of How To Survive Yourself and Patterns to Destroy

"R.C. Lloyd effortlessly weaves faith with healing, her words a balm to soothe the scars and a safe space to feel the complex emotions evoked from living with a chronic illness... A book that opens itself to the hope of life with limitations."

- V.J.Markham, Author of Incantations of a Wild Heart, The Season of Her, and October Falls

This is dedicated to you
as you learn to have grace with yourself

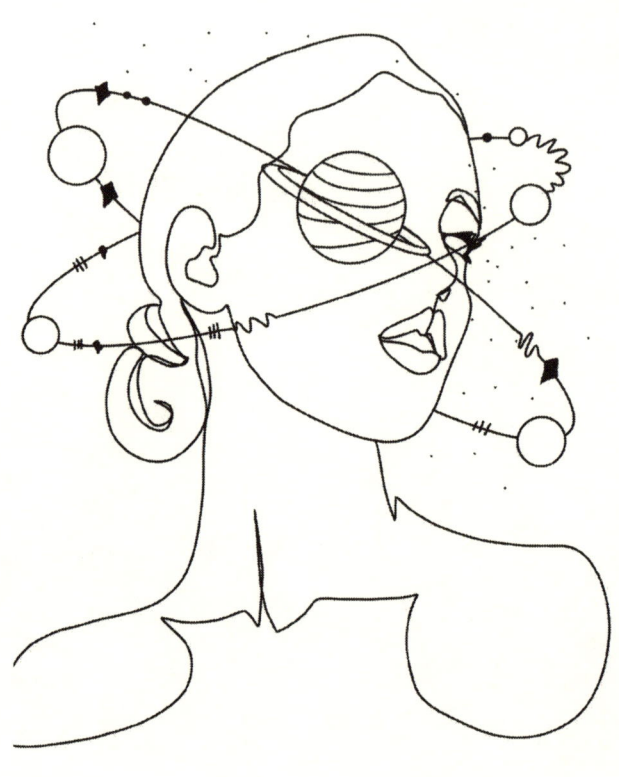

To Do

Have grace with:

- ☐ The body God forged in His Likeness
- ☐ The bones He infused strength into
- ☐ The lungs He breathed stardust into
- ☐ The mind He imbued understanding into
- ☐ The heart He painted oh so much love on

Dear Reader,

I've written these precious poems over a span of three years, but only some reflect where I am now. Many of them are musings, paths I've walked through and come out of, or even inspired by close friends' experiences.

Don't close this book and look at me with pity in your eyes. That's not why I chose to share it. No, this collection is an intimate portrait of what living with a chronic illness can be like. It's a collection of moments: both raw and hopeful. It's about having grace with yourself because of the grace you've been given. So take what you need.

May you feel seen and know you're not alone in whatever you're facing. May you be reminded to keep fighting when it gets hard but also be gentle with yourself when it's too hard. May you have a better understanding of some of the things that people with chronic health conditions face. And may you choose to trust God through it all.

Enjoy this little slice of my heart, but please be gentle.

R.C. Lloyd

A New Definition

Chronic defiance / a balancing act
weightier than a simple attitude of rebellion

Composed of more than 16-year-olds sneaking out
dancing on rooftops / delighting in the dark

Chronic defiance / a battle
where spirit fights body

and wins endurance
for each new day

to breathe and eat
to care and sleep

to stand and dance
to write and speak

Chronic defiance / denying accommodation
to the words Could've / Should've / Would've

chronic defiance

Instead keeping up appearances
even as your body cracks like a glowstick

Making something of the day
while your chest twists with pain and your lungs tighten

Painting your words with kindness
even as your body is cruel

Living with legitimate pains that are signs of nothing
simply vindictive sensations

reminding you of the one thing
you can never forget:

*You are sick
and you will never be better*

Chronic defiance / never a regular occurrence
Why?

Because it's exhausting
and often takes all you have

It leaves you bleeding out / dehydrated
behind for far longer than most find acceptable

Yet it's often the only way to experience moments
your body denied you permission to attend

Sunshine

Existing in sunshine brings joy
But also an exhaustion
A bone weariness that clings to your ankles
Dragging you back as you try to move forward

You live for sunshine moments

The hazy high of a concert
The buzzing room at a party
The first splash at the sea
First dates and gym days
The makeup and confidence of Halloween

You have so little time
But so much to experience

With this knowledge comes fear
The fear that there's not enough time
That you'll never do it all. See it all
Taste it all. Live at all

have you even lived?

chronic defiance

They tell you not to waste time
You'll be old before you know it

They tell you not to waste time
You may never grow old

And that's when it hits you
Burnout coupled with realization
You won't be old before you know it

The gray crown of age?
May never grace your head
Not everyone gets such a prize

Fear drives to packing
Packing sunshine moments in every quiet space
Trying to reach for it all at once

Until the sunshine gives you heatstroke
And your very bones ache
And now I lay me down to sleep

This is why the sun bows to the moon for half the day
And on the seventh day / He rested
You should really do the same

r.c. lloyd

Sunlit Lands

This side of heaven
is messy
you and I are
fragile beings

hearts break
bones fracture
muscles tear
minds shatter

rest in the light of eternity
sprawl out on the carpet
as it streams in through the cracks
let it warm and sustain your weary soul

r.c. lloyd

Rest

I turn away because today needs a courage too heavy
and I packed light this morning

did you know that rest
is not weakness?

It took me a long time to learn that one
because I crave movement and energy and highs

but my body does not
some days it can't carry a tea

much less the courage or hope
needed to do anything more

resting is choosing a future over the present
a demanding feat when living in the moment is everything

still / I honor my body
and unhinged / I rest

to be a force of nature
one must be patient with the storm

r.c. lloyd

The Adrenaline of Anticipation

Even the sunniest of appointment days are darker
Clouds invisible to all but me
Patiently raining tears for hearts

Each diagnostic test
Its own little Schrödinger's box
Anticipation containing both good news and bad news
Simultaneously

The highs of life are when I feel most alive

Dancing / Concerts
Driving in the dark

The terror of stepping off the platform
and flying across the treetops on a wire

But at every appointment / I'm reminded
My favorite words are stable. Uneventful. Quiet.

These are the days I pull my loved ones close

Where Physicality and Emotions Blur

My heart is constantly under renovation
redecorated with fingerprints

I treasure some
while others make my skin crawl

I'll always think of yours first
love in innocence / hands intertwined

Then white coats
literal fingerprints
each a signature of their skill
stitches that keep my heart beating

Then friends
some of whom have passed through my chest
leaving bleeding exit wounds
while others remain (thank you for staying)

Then family
fingerprints as permanent
as the ones you and I pressed into cement
together as children

And men
the many who have pressed thumbprints on my heart
only for them to leave / me to push them out
before they could put down more

I don't know how many more renovations my heart can take
soon enough all the fingerprints will blur
becoming a tragedy of fine lines in my chest

chronic defiance

is it possible to love too much?

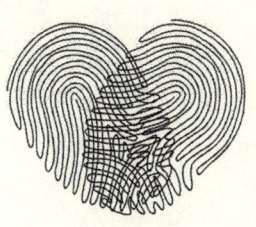

r.c. lloyd

Love / Be Loved

Love is a prayer shawl
tangible actions to wrap yourself in

Armor from the cold
because this world is so cold

Please Persist

With any medical diagnosis:
chronic / terminal / other

Comes dread nesting deep in your bones
an acute awareness of your own mortality

Your hand forced
as your purpose shifts

From planning a retirement
to planning a legacy

You start to say I love you often
and in the most mundane moments

Because you never know when they'll be the last
and they deserve to know just how loved they are

You search for meaning with a newfound desperation
living with more presence and intentionality than before

And treasuring every moment spent
with those you love

You love bigger
and more deeply

And can fluently speak the language of pain
with those you've struggled to understand until now

chronic defiance

You still take some things for granted
and that's okay

You deserve moments where you exist without
the presence of a diagnosis

You're not alone as you peer down the tunnel of time
newly minted fear blurring the edges of your vision

Providing a tearstained look
at a once believed clear future

But the truth is / your future here was never promised
uncertainty is a reality in even the healthiest bodies

Accepting a diagnosis
is choosing to live with intention

Is creating memories to look back on
as things get worse

Because inevitably
things will get worse

*Honor the pain
while refusing to live for it*

*And persist darling
though the darkness threatens to swallow you*

It Only Gets Much Worse

Take a lesson from the queen of the underworld
Bloom in darkness

Citrus in her hair
Kindness on her tongue

Iron in her spin
Pomegranate in her lungs

Darkness behind
Darkness ahead

Still Persephone plants
Never letting the pain define

Even darkness cannot obscure her beauty
Even darkness cannot slow her growth

Ribbons / Needles / Drops of blood
Stain her flowers and rot her fruits

Scars / Bruises / Lingering ghosts
Paint her skin and taunt her soul

Physical / Emotional / Spiritual
Each day a new experience of hell

Still the queen sets a flower crown atop her head
and chooses to cultivate joy in the depths

The phrase
Things will get better

Belongs among
monsters and myths

Guarded from impressionable mortals
by Hades and Cerberus

Platitude masquerading as promise
truly the most treacherous

Who promised you better in this life?
I promise you worse

r.c. lloyd

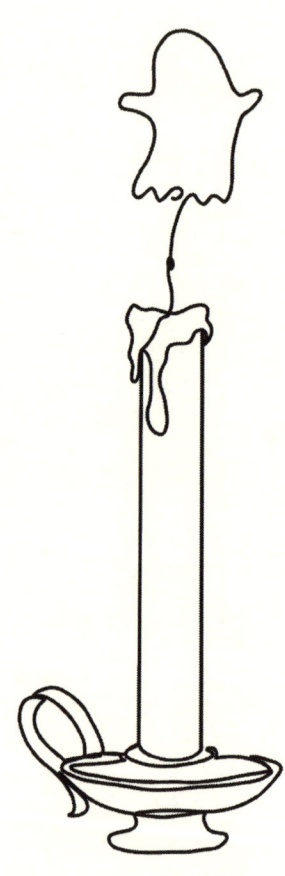

The Wildfire of Pain

Pain isn't always a forest fire
Blazing through our lives
Tearing through plans and growth

sometimes
it's a crackling fireplace
or even wood wick candle

comforting
a familiar friend
one we'd grow cold without

Though if someone else took on
The pain we carry daily
Mercilessly unprepared

They'd believe their world was burning down
Flee from the very moments they'd longed for
And scream into the void

My Drug of Choice

Where do you go to hide?

When the pains are too sharp
The voices too loud
The fears too real

When you have so much to hide from
Considerable pain to escape
Abounding fears to outrun

When the back of your orange bottles caution
Against traditional methods of drowning
A stiff drink. A quick hit.

I chase the runner's high: endorphins
My gym membership: my lifeline
The great outdoors: the only place I'm ever truly free

chronic defiance

There's something therapeutic
About stepping onto the dance floor
Or those first deep breaths at the top of a mountain

About lacing up your climbing shoes
And gripping the rock wall so tightly
Everything else falls away

About leaving your problems at the door
As you unroll your yoga mat
And feel the stress melt off you

To exercise is to condition your body
Silence the voices
Soothe the soul

I've searched for a quarter of a century
And can say with confidence
Exercise is the most powerful drug I've tried

r.c. lloyd

sedatephobia:

Fear / dread / a deep aversion to silence. Derived from the Greek words Sedate' (silent)' and Phobos (the personification of fear).

Sedatephobia

I am most at peace when I cannot hear my own heartbeat

Ticking like the clock in the crocodile
Taunting Captain Hook

A relentless reminder of mortality
Counting down the seconds to death

My Spotify Wrapped was over 100 thousand minutes
more than all my friends (172,501 to be exact)

A December reminder that I wrap myself in sound
Anything to retreat

Anything to drown out the
Maddening

Everpresent
Beat of my own heart

I am most at peace when I cannot hear my own heartbeat

r.c. lloyd

Blessed Assurance

Promise me you'll cling to hope

Your entire universe hinges on the word
And what it means to you

Is it a pinky promise that they'll always be there
Whispered plans between lovers
Wishful thinking about what's next

Or is it an assurance unwavering
Because the One who gives it
Is the same One who breathed starlight into existence?

I pray you choose the latter

r.c. lloyd

The Hymnal Of My Upbringing

I was raised on the blade of eternity
Taught to see everything along it
Reminded not to forget Your faithfulness
Great is Thy Faithfulness

This is the sky in me
boundless expanse
dotted with forget-me-nots
in full bloom / beaming starlight

Stardust in my lungs
ashes of a collapsed star in my veins
tragedy and rebirth
pulsing as one

Ancient constellations
Childlike / standing before
Ageless God
Age to Age He Stands

r.c. lloyd

Lilacs

There is a heavy beauty
in the mere impermanence of hospital flowers

A taste of life perched on sterilized nightstands
a touch of wildness permitted in a controlled environment

Here today / gone tomorrow
they fade / wither / die

Much like the patients they lend companionship to
the impermanence makes them precious

The shared weight of withering
the shared burden of a shortened life

Stop and smell the flowers
spend time with your loved ones

Take real photographs / develop the memories
clutch them a little tighter

One day I'll plant a lilac tree
a permanent fixture for me to clip impermanence from

But for now
please bring me wild lilacs next time I'm in the hospital

r.c. lloyd

Eternal / Temporal

Lightning strikes somewhere
and we're mere mortals once more
This is tragedy's tongue

Our suffering made temporary
Our pain flashes by
Our God / eternal

Hope lends strength
And we cling to the impermanence of pain
Coupled with the promise of eternal glory

Trace the hurricane with your weary eyes
Learn to live and love within the storm
Even as pain fights you for ownership of every moment

The sharp bolt may never dissipate in this life
But the knife dulls over time
As you inch closer to the endless

Your moments are numbered
Decimals in light of eternity
Soon enough you too will be a memory

Another Year / A Gift

Wish me a quarter century
But don't wish me a quarter life

Don't you dare
Assign time

I may have far less
Than you know

Your passing phrase
An act of hubris

A cosmic responsibility
Claimed by mere mortal

The true length of a lifetime known
Only once it ends

Treasure the time
Every single dragging moment

The beautiful ones too
Because they are numbered

But they are most certainly not
Numbered by you or I

The One who fashioned
Time in His hands

The Giver of Life
Alone gets that privilege

chronic defiance

Not us

r.c. lloyd

Turn Your Face / Face The Wind

Surrender is to hold everything with
open hands / open hearts / open expectations

patiently letting opportunities
pass through with the wind

waiting for the one that
stays / loops around your fingers / holds on

Darling
Hold on

Stillness

In stillness / we grow

in faith
in hope
in love

Our persistence / a palm
whipping wildly in the hurricane
while holding fast by its roots
a faithful fixture in the storm

Our patience / a painting
the artist blending colors to tell a story
the product unclear and slow
the process the true purpose

Our prayers / many waters
powerful and capable of calm or rage
strong enough to reach the heavens
yet quiet enough to remain in our hearts

Our peace / not ours
Peace in the work of Christ
Peace resting in His promises
Peace with God

Dearest
Sit in stillness with quiet expectation
Be at peace my sisters
Be at peace my brothers

This is the Strengthening of Self

Your language has softened over time
As have your memories of pain

The words with which you describe yourself
Your circumstances
And most importantly / the souls in your life
Have significantly warmed

Melting from bitterness to kindness
When held over the candle of time

Gaping wounds soften to scars
That inform your future

Grieving heartbreak
softens to enduring love

Physical pain
softens to empathy

Anger at injustice
softens to action

Regret
softens to wisdom

Fear of loss
softens to treasuring time

After all
we have so little time anyways

chronic defiance

Is the softening of self
The strengthening of character?

Softening is healing
Softening is loss

Softening is losing the bitterness
You wore as a badge of honor
Pointing it out to those who didn't comment on it
Stretching the wound every so often so it didn't close
Wearing things that showed your scarred soul

Why / if not to take pride in your sin.
Is not pride alone a sin?

Softening is losing the edge in your words
Your language lined with bitterness

Edged with a darkness
That comes only from shining a light
On suffering and pain and darkness

Losing your words laced
With an unkindness thanks to an injustice

Softening is losing a part of yourself that was so sharp
It could slice through time
And make you bleed as though the wound was fresh

This is the Strengthening of Self (cont.)

You loved how sharp your soul was
~~Still do~~

But darling perhaps
You were sharpening all the wrong parts of your soul

Iron sharpens iron
This still rings true
And is the mark of someone worth keeping

Someone with a forge in their soul
And healing in their words

Continue to search for souls who sharpen your faith
Wisdom / Empathy / Kindness

And most importantly / sharpen your love
But search also for souls who soften yours

Embrace the duality of humanity

Softening characteristics
That make you curl into your pain

While sharpening characteristics
That radiate light

(This is the strengthening of self)

r.c. lloyd

Violet / Violence / Violins

Did you see love and pain mingling at the symphony?
flirting as though they were alone

hues floating as notes
bruises dancing through time

they say scars come with living
but so too does joy

in music / in color
in laughter / in love

be informed by pain
but act in love

r.c. lloyd

Composition

You are crescendo
Breathing and beloved

Heartbeat composed
of hymns and prayers

Kintsugi

Fissures and fragments
That's all we are anyways

Broken vessels in various stages
Of breakage and healing

Too many mend alone
Concealing pain as it scabs over

Hiding from loved ones and strangers alike
Suffering in silence

Rebuking the very communities
God designed us for

Darling you deserve better
We all do

Kintsugi is the treatment of scars
With a golden salve

One that shines in the light
One that's reflected in your actions and words

Welcoming your scars onto your skin
Writing your pain into your story

Healing is painting kindness along your jagged edges
Pressing them together

Holding them until they're strong enough to stay
But doing so with dignity over shame

Creating art that inspires self-worth from pain
Sharing it until no one else is isolated in the same way

Your scars / brokenness / healing process
Are as much a part of your identity as your soul

Invite community into your heart
To walk with you as you claim and decorate your scars

r.c. lloyd

It Can Be Done

Have you ever seen a woman piece herself together?
Pressing fragments to one another
Painting grace in the cracks
Blowing patience as they dry

r.c. lloyd

Mend As You May

your battle scars may not be visible
your wounds painted under your skin
but they're still there

each fight takes a toll on your body
spit out the blood and rest your aching bones

be gentle with your broken body
be kind to your wounded heart
be quiet with your traumatized spirit

rest and let rest wash over you
recover and let recovery mend you

grit your teeth
stitch yourself back together
and rest

just because no one can see your scars
doesn't mean they don't deserve to be cared for

Yours Alone

Refuse anyone's definition of your scars

Don't let people thank you for them
Tell you they made you
Stronger
More modest
Kinder
Beautiful even

That's no one's place

You alone decide how to speak about your scars
The tone with which the words leave your mouth

You may just hate them
You have every right

They may be seeds
from which bitterness took root

They may be fears
Taunting you with your weaknesses

They may be shadows
Where your insecurities dance

They may be art
You display with pride
Delighting
in the twisted colors and shapes

chronic defiance

Or they may be your testimony
The story of God's faithfulness in your life
Penned on your skin

Healing Truths

Christian platitudes
taunt
encircle
ensnare me

Wrapping each honey dripping word
around my wrists and ankles

They draw no blood but slow me down
holding me prisoner to false assurances

Everything will work out
You'll get better
You'll get through this
He only gives you as much as you can handle
He'll take away your pain
He'll rescue you from your illness

I hate that these words
promise things my Savior does not

I hate that these words
make my Savior look weak

chronic defiance

He is strong

And it is only because of that truth
that I am strong

Strong enough to wash off
the sticky words of this world

And wrap myself in Scriptural Truths
read by those of sound mind

Written on my chest
over every scar

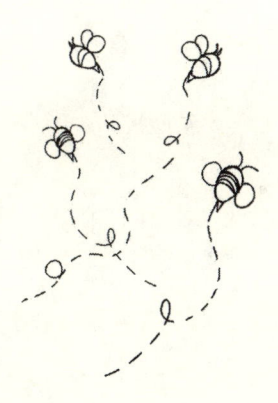

r.c. lloyd

To My Parents

You're the reason I don't ask
how could a loving God…
Or *why is there pain and suffering*

I don't question God's fairness
an incomprehensible thing
that's been the downfall of many

Instead / I arm myself with
each word spoken over me
through each year of my life

Your prayers are my armor
Your faith is my armor
Your love is my armor

How could a loving God…
is the wrong question
to be asking in this broken world

Instead / you taught me to ask
*how can I take my pain and suffering
and use them to help others heal?*

r.c. lloyd

Romans 12:15

Rejoice with those who rejoice, weep with those who weep.

Hold My Hand

My suffering doesn't need to fit within your worldview
It's okay if you're at a loss

It's okay not to be optimistic
It's okay not to have all the answers (or any even)
It's okay to not read scriptures and platitudes
It's okay to not preach / promise / pray

Paul calls us to share
In one another's joy and sufferings alike

Just be here
Listen to me
Sing to me
Hold me

Speak of the places I've been
Dream of the places I'll go

Just be present
Hold my hand
And don't let go
That's all I ask

Dearest
please don't let go

r.c. lloyd

Tiny Dancer

Learn to dance in the storm

A platitude that unflinchingly excludes
us whose bodies collapse
at the so-called universal expression of dance

I aged in a hospital
hidden under the shelter of books
living lives I thought I'd never live

Do you remember Angelina Ballerina? I do.

My heart is stronger now
so I dance for the tiny ballerina who wept
as peers raised their graceful legs towards the sky

I dance in celebration of my body

in gratitude of legs
that carry my weight

lungs
that hold enough breath to make it through a song

balance
that lets me spin without collapsing

Take my hand
Dance with me

But don't you dare tell people to dance
in the midst in their storms

r.c. lloyd

A Celebration of You

My darling
you're asking all the wrong questions again

It's not *why can't I keep up*
or *how could my body let me down*

It's not *how do I fade these scars*
or *why am I always in so much pain*

Instead ask *what did my body do for me today*
and celebrate the movement

Ask *how can I care for my body*
and *when can I make time for a rest*

Ask *what have I eaten today*
and *have I been kind to myself*

Train your mind
to appreciate what your body *can do*

Train your mind
to focus more on caring than comparing

Appreciate how your carefully stitched self
is a vessel for joy and experiencing life

Celebrate this body
that God molded specifically for your soul

A Permission Slip

Friendships among the chronically ill
Lend to inappropriate jests in public

About taking your drugs
Being high

Mixing drugs and alcohol
And of course / stabbing yourself

While we make jokes in one breath
We encourage one another with the next

I take medication for my heart
Why wouldn't you take it for your mind?

Check your sugar
Here's a juice box

What's your heart rate?
I'll slow down for you

Your lips are purple
Take a break

Here's a heat pack
I'm proud of you for protecting your energy

We've learned that
If you don't make time to rest

Your body will force you to
At the most inconvenient of times

chronic defiance

So stop
Breathe

Rest
Pray

Care for your brain
Care for your body

Watch as medicine strengthens you
A gift that sustains you for longer

Your medication is empowering
Don't entertain anyone who tries to tell you otherwise

Fix your highs in public
Stop to medicate

Be the last one up the mountain
Still celebrate at the top

Stab yourself
And defy their expectations

My friends and I give you permission
To make people uncomfortable

Because they don't know what it takes
To maintain a disintegrating body

r.c. lloyd

Dirt / Love

Gaze with me at the heavens
Watch as centuries dance by

Let me lay my head on your chest
Let the stars rain down on us

Excruciating fireballs
Radiating beauty

Destruction and healing
Encapsulated in a speck of spacedust

This moment is a culmination
Of stardust and sovereignty

You are a culmination
Of dirt and love

You Got To Live

To my elders
You may think it's funny

But every time you jest about turning 30 again
Dye your hair to conceal the grays
And refuse to share your age

The knife in my chest twists a little deeper
A cruel jab as you go beyond taking age for granted

And actually lament
Something I crave

Your salt and pepper hair
crowns

Crowns of experience
Beyond my capacity

Imbued with wisdom and grace
That only come with age

I long to wear a crown as you do

To walk through life long enough
That my rickety bones are infused with
The same wisdom and grace

chronic defiance

Don't you know how blessed you are?

You've gotten to live many years
That I may never enter
My heart aches for the years I may never walk

I wish you could see yourself as I do
Kings and Queens
Ones that get luckier with every precious year

You get to live

r.c. lloyd

Acceptance

Oh to soar
To have a body that doesn't rebel at every turn
That instead replies to my pleas with energy
That's eager to experience

Roller coasters
Cliff diving
Bungee jumping
Hangliding

As close as the human body can come to flying
Yet too hard on my fragile body

I'd crumble to ash
Leaving a trail of dust in my path
And heart pounding in my throat
Until it ruptures

I'm sick
This I know
But I'm sick of it defining me
Of it being the reason behind my refusals

Part of accepting a diagnosis is accepting
I'll never nosedive from a cliff
Skim the salty sea with my wingspan
And pitch back upwards to taste the clouds

Oh how I long to taste the clouds

Limitless

The human experience is measured in limits
I know mine

Still I press my face to the window and ask
What's it like?

Not to be confined by the limits
of your own body?

Not to hear and fear
your own heartbeat?

To fill your lungs with all the mountain air
God designed them to hold?

To push your limits
without sacrificing your future?

To fly down a mountain
without the cold searing through your bones?

To bend and not break?
To have a body that empowers you to explore?

Wait
Don't tell me

I don't know if my weak heart could carry
The knowledge without the practice

Everyone has their limits
Mine just feel more confining than most

Limitless (cont.)

Still

Physical limits taught me to value
Limitless truths

Transcendent peace
(beyond understanding)

Boundless grace
(far more than I deserve)

Unceasing hope
(eagerly waiting on the Lord)

Immeasurable faith
(certainty of what I cannot see)

Unconditional love
(loving because He loved me first)

Discovering my limits were bound only
To the physical realm

Was akin to learning I could fly

That's why I'm so generous with *I love you*

My limits have taught me
To be generous with the limitless

r.c. lloyd

chronic defiance

r.c. lloyd

Acknowledgments

While so many people have helped shape my heart, these are the people, without whom Chronic Defiance wouldn't exist.

First and foremost: The Belletrists, my writing group of faithful and inspiring friends. You three are the embodiment of kindred spirits and how I love being a woman. You've been a constant encouragement as I've prepared to share this piece of my heart.

Sara, thank you for designing the layout, illustrations, and cover of my dreams. You took this collection from document to book. Erin, thank you for beta reading and reassuring me this collection is beautiful. And Jenni, thank you for bouncing poems back and forth with me. I thank God for female friendships, most specifically each of yours. You're my flower crown fastest friends.

Faith, my friend, my sister, my beloved beta reader. Thank you for walking with me through many of the moments that inspired this collection.

Sam, one who's grown next to me and pushed me to finally share this. Thank you. I've loved being a part of your healing journey as much as you are in mine.

Ryan, the first one to start calling me a poet. Thank you. Your reflections on my words pointed out more beauty in them than I would've seen alone.

Jenna, my loyal friend and sister. There've been many days when you've been way more excited about this collection than I was. Thank you for your confidence in me.

Ben, a constant support. I wrote the Dear Reader letter after you mentioned the idea in a conversation. And the collection wouldn't be the same without it. Thank you for continually asking what God's doing in my life. Never stop asking people that.

Kayla, a literal light in my life. Thank you for constantly demonstrating Christ's love and making me laugh. You are the sun.

chronic defiance

Lydia and Karyn, the besties. The best cheerleaders a girl could ask for. You've been next to me from the start, looping your arms through mine and pulling me through this life. Thank you.

Rain, my ride or die. You make sure I always see the daylight. Thank you for that. Things will get brighter for us both. If not in this life, then in the next.

Cassie, my OG chronic girlie. You've gotten a front row seat to my highs and lows. Especially the lows. Thank you for all the 3am meals, dances, and champagne glasses.

And my parents. Thank you for raising me to walk in The Lord. Thank you for carrying me whenever I couldn't walk on my own. You're the reason I am planted firmly in God. You're the reason I write of His faithfulness.

r.c. lloyd

About the Author

R.C. Lloyd is a writer and poet from Upstate NY, whose experience growing up with an artificial heart valve and pacemaker contributes to her #ownvoices perspective. She wrote Chronic Defiance to provide a glimpse into life with a chronic illness and to come alongside those who walk it daily. She's currently working on multiple speculative fiction books, but Chronic Defiance is the first book to make her an author. No small feat with all those characters battling for her attention.

r.c. lloyd

Index

Praise for Chronic Defiance	3
Dedication	5
To Do	7
Dear Reader,	9
A New Definition	10
Sunshine	12
Sunlit Lands	15
Rest	17
The Adrenaline of Anticipation	19
Where Physicality and Emotions Blur	20
Love / Be Loved	23
Please Persist	24
It Only Gets Much Worse	26
The Wildfire of Pain	29
My Drug of Choice	30
Sedatephobia	33
Blessed Assurance	35
The Hymnal Of My Upbringing	37
Lilacs	39
Eternal / Temporal	41
Another Year / A Gift	42
Turn Your Face / Face The Wind	45
Stillness	46
This is the Strengthening of Self	48
This is the Strengthening of Self (cont.)	50
Violet / Violence / Violins	53
Composition	55
Kintsugi	56
It Can Be Done	59
Mend As You May	61
Yours Alone	62
Healing Truths	64
To My Parents	67
Hold My Hand	69
Tiny Dancer	71
A Celebration of You	73
A Permission Slip	74
Dirt / Love	77
You Got To Live	78
Acceptance	81
Limitless	82
Limitless (cont.)	84
Acknowledgments	89
About the Author	93

Golden Salve Press
Copyright © 2023 by R.C. Lloyd. All rights reserved.
Paperback ISBN: 979-8-9889307-0-9

All rights reserved. No part of this publication may be reproduced, stored in a retrieval system or transmitted in any form or by any means (electronic, mechanical, photocopying, recording, or otherwise) without the written permission of the author and publisher. However, sharing photos and lines is encouraged so long as the author is credited.

Instagram: beca.poetry

Formatting / Cover design and Illustration © Sara Francis
SF Publishing & Media | Sara-Francis.com

Author Photo © Rain Paul

Scripture quotations are from the ESV® Bible (The Holy Bible, English Standard Version®), copyright© 2001 by Crossway, a publishing ministry of Good News Publishers. Used by permission. All rights reserved. The ESV text may not be quoted in any publication made available to the public by a Creative Commons license. The ESV may not be translated in whole or in part into any other language.

Made in the USA
Middletown, DE
08 December 2023